YOUR KNOWLEDGE HAS VALUE

- We will publish your bachelor's and master's thesis, essays and papers

- Your own eBook and book - sold worldwide in all relevant shops

- Earn money with each sale

Upload your text at www.GRIN.com and publish for free

Bibliographic information published by the German National Library:

The German National Library lists this publication in the National Bibliography; detailed bibliographic data are available on the Internet at http://dnb.dnb.de .

This book is copyright material and must not be copied, reproduced, transferred, distributed, leased, licensed or publicly performed or used in any way except as specifically permitted in writing by the publishers, as allowed under the terms and conditions under which it was purchased or as strictly permitted by applicable copyright law. Any unauthorized distribution or use of this text may be a direct infringement of the author s and publisher s rights and those responsible may be liable in law accordingly.

Imprint:

Copyright © 2017 GRIN Verlag, Open Publishing GmbH
Print and binding: Books on Demand GmbH, Norderstedt Germany
ISBN: 9783668461536

This book at GRIN:

http://www.grin.com/en/e-book/367675/from-rags-to-riches-differences-and-parallels-as-regards-to-the-foundation

Lis Voll

"From Rags to Riches"? Differences and Parallels as Regards to the Foundation and Future Development of American and German Enterprises

GRIN Publishing

GRIN - Your knowledge has value

Since its foundation in 1998, GRIN has specialized in publishing academic texts by students, college teachers and other academics as e-book and printed book. The website www.grin.com is an ideal platform for presenting term papers, final papers, scientific essays, dissertations and specialist books.

Visit us on the internet:

http://www.grin.com/

http://www.facebook.com/grincom

http://www.twitter.com/grin_com

Gymnasium Haus Overbach

Extended Project

„From rags to riches"? Differences and parallels as regards the foundation and future development of American and German enterprises

Grade Level: Q1.2
Course: Lk / E / Kä

Date of submission: 05th of April, 2017

Table of contents

1. Introduction 3
2. Frame Conditions 4
    2.1. Political and environmental situations 4
        2.1.1. Political and environmental situation America 4
        2.1.2. Political and environmental situation Germany 5
    2.2. Demographics 7
        2.2.1. Demographics America 7
        2.2.2. Demographics Germany 8
3. Society and Culture 9
    3.1. school and education 9
        3.1.1. school and education America 9
        3.1.2. School and education Germany 10
    3.2. Culture 12
        3.2.1. Culture America 12
        3.2.2. Culture Germany 13
4. Conclusion 14
5. Summary 15
6. Bibliography 17
Statement 19

1. Introduction

Companies are the driving force of a country's economy. Besides the fact that the innovations improve the standard of living by making life much more comfortable and easy, they create new jobs which lead to economic growth. In addition, the national income increases due to a higher rate of tax revenue. A stable economy with a wide variety of businesses is one reason for prosperity in the country. Therefore, it is a country's aim to attract (young) people with new and passionate ideas who aim to set up their own businesses – these people are known as entrepreneurs. Moreover the belief is that even with a low budget it is possible to make money and become a millionaire. Especially in America the "the American Dream" is still in mind.

"From rags to riches"? Is this saying still true? Can people rely on what is always said and believe in the "unlimited opportunities" they are indirectly promised? On the contrary the Federal Republic of Germany is aware of the potential of the newcomers in business. With much effort, Germany tries to create promising surroundings for entrepreneurs. America, however is a giant, regarding geographical size and the size of the markets that are open to any potential founders. Is Germany even a good alternative to the well–known America, "land of dreams"?

This extended project focusses on the differences and parallels in regard to the foundation and future development of American and German enterprises. After comparing the social and market factors of these two countries, the reader will be given an answer to the question "From rags to riches?" –a true statement for Germany as well as America. In this project, the main focus is on the product and innovation based start–ups.

2. Frame Conditions
2.1. Political and environmental situations
2.1.1. Political and environmental situation America

The 'GDP'(Gross Domestic Product) transfers the health of a country's economy into numbers. All products and services that have been produced in a specific period of time are calculated to a total dollar value. On the one hand, the number makes a comparison between states possible, one the other hand it gives information about the size of the economy which is directly linked to the performance of the entrepreneurs[1] (Conway, Managing and Shaping innovation). A high GDP indicates that the entrepreneurial activity is enhancing as the market grows to a larger extent. Moreover, it means security for the entrepreneurs as it is unlikely that a sudden destruction of the market occurs and therefore will lead to a forced shutdown of the business. The Gross Domestic Product also provides information about the expenditure of the citizens. Especially for the innovation driven start–ups, a population of the financial wealth is of great significance as they are only able to sell their products if the population has the materialistic prosperity to make these expenditures. Another aspect that has to be taken into consideration is innovation. Innovation means the "commercialisation of technological change"[2] (Rosenberg).

The Unites States of America has a population of 319.0 million people who live on 9,826,675 km²[3] (Kelley). Being the third largest country as regards the number of citizens, the entrepreneurs profit of the numerous markets they have access to. The size is advantageous - especially for founders who try to get into the market with niche products. In addition, for people of foreign origin that factor is often the reason for a relocation as that economy is very favorable to position new investments. However, the entrepreneurs have to be aware that a larger market also indicates a greater number of market participants who embody further competitors. This assumption is borne out by "World Economic Forum Global Competitive Ranking" in which America is on the third rank of 140 countries[4] (World Economic Forum). The American market is continuously prospering which is an exceedingly positive aspect with regard to the entrepreneurial options. America's physical infrastructure is on a high level in comparison to other 62 countries[5] (Kelley). That result implies that the entrepreneurs can

---

[1] e.g. Conway, p. 114
[2] e.g. Rosenberg Inside the Black Box: Technology and Economics p. 16
[3] e.g. Global Report p.112
[4] e.g World Economic Forum, United States
[5] e.g. Global Report p.112

make use of a widely extended infrastructure, an online network and transport facilities. The infrastructure is the essential fundament, especially when the entrepreneurs want to extend the business.

Examining the degree of innovation, the USA ranks 4th in the overall ranking in 2016. To secure the innovation, the founders intend to file a patent application. That degree of innovation can therefore be examined in the patent application by origin. In the total comparison, the United State rank highly the 6th place[6] (Pinkwart) .Therefore, it can be stated that America's economy prospers due to the high quantity of unique innovations. Another important factor is the cluster structure in the United States. Clusters, like the world famous Silicon Valley and the city New York City, are defined as a geographical close group of enterprises and institutes which are connected with each other through similarities. The effect is a local competitive situation and an advantage of the economy. Moreover, the entrepreneurs get easier access to knowledge and an exchange of experiences. The clustered environment is especially widespread in the United States.

The U.S. plays a major role in the international trade system and favors a demolition of trade barriers and free trade agreements. Among them are the North American Free Trade Agreement (NAFTA), which is a federation with Canada and Mexico. The United States is also an active member of the World Trade Organization (WTO). These trade agreements enable the entrepreneurs to open their offerings to the world. The chances to make more profit increase[7]. (Schumpeter)

2.1.2. Political and environmental situation Germany

Germany is regarded as a country with a stable economy. The total population of the federal state is 82.150,7 million. Germany, which is at the center of Europe, measures 356,840 square kilometers. The GDP is 3,472,570,4 USD dollar and therefore the 4th largest in the world and is growing with a rate of 1.8 percent. In addition, the unemployment rate remains low[8] (Germany Country Factfile). Having these numbers in the international comparison, Germany stands out and is an excellent fundament for entrepreneurial activities. A good economy "pulls" employable people into self–employment. That effect is considered as the "pull factor". In addition, Germany is part of the EU, thus all of their FTA are linked directly to the EU. Being in the EU means trading

---

6 e.g. Analyse des Gründungsgeschehen in Deutschland p.16
7 e.g. Schumpeter: The Theory of economic development p. 51
8 e.g. Germany Country Factfile

without barriers. That entails a reduction of cost and therefore a making of more profit is the result. 62% of businesses say that cost is the main reason for moving abroad[9] (Byrne). That makes Germany favorable as a county to set up for example a logistic business.

Moreover, the trade agreement CETA with Canada has stood as a political agreement since October 2013. Furthermore, the trade agreement with T-TIP with the United States is a positive agreement as the main benefit for entrepreneurs is the simplified international trade and the founders have access to international markets[10] (Office of the United States Trade Representative). Germany is connected to the wider world – but also the inner infrastructure contributes to the entrepreneurial activity. The term "physical infrastructure refers to the basic physical structures required for an economy to function and survive, such as transportation networks, a power grid", transportation networks and postal and telecommunications services[11] (Ascher). In a ranking that compares the countries in the quality of infrastructure, Germany scores the third rank[12] (Schwab).

In another survey where experts had to examine the strength and weaknesses of the framework condition, the physical infrastructure ranks the first place with 83%[13] (Sternberg). Infrastructure enhances connectivity and links that facilitate the recognition of entrepreneurial opportunities and the ability of entrepreneurs to actualise those opportunities. Another important aspect is that an extensive infrastructure encourages the birth and growth and development of small enterprises. For Germany, a developed infrastructure is essential as the start–up sectors in 2015 were 29% personal services and 37% business services. One in five business founders are established in the digital market. Customers therefore get access to their offering through digital devices[14] (Metzger). It is in the digital markets that founders profit most, using the well networked infrastructure in Germany that gives all citizens the possibility of access to Internet.

Innovation and intervention are both crucial aspects that have to be examined in the founding scene. The invention is the discovery of a new product or finding new way to produce products. Innovation on the contrary is defined as follows: It is the process

---

9 e.g. Byrne 'New Entrepreneurship' p.3
10 e.g. Office of the United States
11 e.g. Wolinski, John AQA A Level Business 1 Third Edition p.20
12 e.g. Schwab: The Global Competitiveness Report p.21
13 e.g. Brixy: Global Entrepreneurship Monitor p.20
14 e.g. Metzger: "KfW-Start-up Monitor 2016" p.4

of transferring an invention into a product that customers will buy. The latter is especially important for entrepreneurs as they will only make profit if they sell their products[15] (Wolinski). In Germany, the number of innovative founders rose by 6% to 95,000 persons. Therefore it can be said that Germany has experienced an increasing quality of innovation. A positive correlation has been determined between innovation occurrence and economic growth.

2.2. Demographics
2.2.1. Demographics America

In order to investigate the entrepreneurial environment, demographic coherences are a crucial aspect in investigating the entrepreneurial environment. Before investigating enterprises from the economical point of view, the entrepreneurs themselves have to be scrutinised. Gender, age and ethnicity are the central aspects in this examination as a person is categorised in these three aspects. To understand America's population at the present time, we have to take a step back and must have a look at the first few generations who have lived in the "land of milk and honey". America was established by migrants that have come to the new explored country with the undeniable dream to create a new existence. Through work and effort, contracts and institutions, America gained prestige and a reputation as a land with the unspoken promise of having a real chance to be really involved and part of the American Dream. Down to the present day, the immigrants contribute to the American culture and business status in versatile ways. More than 7% of the adult immigrant population owns a business as their main source of income. Compared to the 5.8% of the Native-Born in America, the number is proves to be true that the Immigrants make a contribution business culture[16] (Robert W. Fairlie). In the United States, the reputation of the entrepreneurial active immigrant is a highly regarded one and from this it follows the enforced entrepreneurial spirit among the previously foreigners.

A striking aspect when analysing the demographics of a nation, is factor of education. In America, there is just one educational path. You either have a High School or College diploma or less than a High School degree. After a quick overview of the graphic, it is noticeable that the number of business owners decreases, regardless of the presence of a degree. However, what does have an impact is the scholastic career: In 2015 33% of people who are business owners had a college degree, 29.5% a High School degree and in 37.5% of the cases the owner's degree was less than High School and

---

15 e.g. John et al.: AQA A Level Business 1 Third Edition p.20
16 e.g. Robert Fairlie: "The Kauffmann Index" p. 33

other degree[17] (Robert W. Fairlie). The numbers don't exhibit much of a difference. Therefore, another aspect that has to be mention is that there is still a chance to succeed even if your scholastic career is not well-advanced.

The "gender – issue" is still a widely discussed topic in and outside of the business world. After having had a look at the line chart, the figure conveys a clear message. 63.2% of the owners are male, solely 36.8% are females[18] (Kelley). These number should not prevent any woman from starting a business. There are no fewer opportunities chances but some women tend to give up their self – assumption and confidence.

2.2.2. Demographics Germany

The facts and figures of the German demographics provide further insight into the foundation activities of the German population. In the first instance, it is important to investigate the age group. People aged 25-34 dominate the entrepreneurial market. 34% of the total quantity lie within that age group. The older the people become, the less likely they become to be the head of a start - up. Even though 22% of the German population are citizens are 55-64 years old, only 8% account to the number of entrepreneurship. On the other hand, the young generation between 18 and 24 years is very active. They contribute with 16% to the total amount[19] (Pinkwart).The median age is at 29.1 years, showing that the market is especially prosperous for young and middle aged people who are willing to change their ideas into a business idea. The difference between man and woman in this field of work is still large. Compared to 71.3% men, the 28.7% that women represent just a minority. The under-representation affects the founder scene negatively as many young women let the opportunity pass by and the potential remains unused (Kelley).

Another factor of high importance to characterise is the educational aspect. Comparing the 32% with academic qualifications and 47% with professional and vocational qualifications, the 20% of people with no qualifications seems low[20] (Metzger). People with a low educational background are especially likely to attempt a business because of the lack of alternative income source. Undereducated people are at significantly higher risk to slip into poverty. By starting a business the dream of success is a driving factor. However, the majority of innovation based start-ups are founded by educated people. The latest numbers (2016) reveal that 184,000 people an d therefore 22% of

---

17 e.g. Fairly "The Kauffmann Index" p.36
18 e.g. Global Entrepreneurship Monitor p.73
19 e.g. Pinkwart: Analyse des Gründungsgeschehens in Deutschland p.7
20 e.g. Metzger, Dr Georg. "KfW-Start-up Monitor 2016 p.6

the total quantity had an immigration background. Taking these numbers into consideration with total amount of people with German roots, the number is considered as particularly high. This can be lined to the aspect previously examined. Foreign people seek the chances to get involved in the German economy and gain prosperity with a entrepreneurial activity.

3. Society and Culture
3.1. school and education
3.1.1. school and education America

The foundation of every developed culture is the system of education which consists of acquiring basic knowledge in the form of facts but more important learning skills such as understanding correlations at a complex level. Linking these two basic elements, a person's mind-set can develop to its highest potential. The school system in the United States differs from the European System. The young children from age 3-5 are enrolled in the kindergarten, then the children attend until the age of eleven the Elementary School. From the 12th grade they attend middle school. The penultimate step in the education system is the upper secondary school education where children are enrolled until year 17. After a successful graduation, the American youth, similar to German, is qualified to go to university, the college or the community college. In view of these facts, the following two aspects are most essential: Firstly, there is just one prescribed educational pathway. Unlike the German "Gymnasium", the more intelligent students attend the advanced courses in order to meet the requirements of the personal learning performance. However, due to the system the student is given more freedom when it comes to making decisions about what to learn.

A 16 year old student, who has attended an American School comments as follows: "[The students] make decisions about what interests they wish to explore, and they can change that decision if they discover they do not care for it"[21] With regard to the economic education, there are also courses with the main focus on economics. Statistics, Business Math, Personal Finance and Investing and Financial Management are listed in the school curriculum. The logical result of this is the assumption that pupils that are guided towards the economic field, are later on more likely to be positively tuned when it comes to the career option of being an entrepreneur. In addition, it is important to mention that American citizens in general have the image of the successful business

---

21 Isabel Schueppel, interview http://www.gac-foundation.org/2015/06/24/american-schools-vs-german-schools/ 25.3.17

starter in mind: Steve Jobs, Mark Zuckerberg, Henry Ford – accomplishers of the American Dream. Right from the start the students are fed with stories of adventures and inventors[22] (Cornwall).

Moreover, it is important to submit unambiguous statements with statistics. The American Entrepreneurial education at school stage scores 3.5 points and is therefore above the average of 3.1 points[23] (Kelley). Nevertheless, at post school stage the bar chart indicates a decrease. With 4.4 points the USA is just under the average score. Another survey which compares the G 20 countries in education and training proves that the US is on the leading position[24] (Sedov).This brings us to another issue. A link can be drawn between investment in education and the Gross Domestic Product Growth. A survey by HHL compares the expenditure for education depending on the GDP of the country. New Zealand is the leading, closely followed by the US.

3.1.2. School and education Germany

The German reformer Wilhelm von Humboldt was one of the main initiators countenancing the government towards introducing reforms in the education system. These policies were the reaction to the defeat against Napoleon in 1806. Humboldt's vision was the progression of a population with a holistic education. Particularly the development of the emotional and intellectual faculty was regarded as a particularly important value. In the early days this concept was implemented solely in grammar schools, however after a short period of time these idealistic education concepts spread all over the country. Yet there were no lessons in the field of economy[25] (Burrow). The question rises as to why the educational concerns of developing economic knowledge is still absent in many federal states. Today as well as then its usefulness is doubted. Therefore, there was no interest of an integration into the school curriculum.

Politicians and those in charge have to look beyond the borders of the 19th century. Entrepreneurial activities start from the very first school day. The lock is the understanding of the word in all its facets – the financial and economic education can be illustrated as the key. The German school system is lacking this key. In a personal assessment in which entrepreneurs had to rate the start- and framework condition, over 50% rated the German education from E to F.

---

22 Jeff Cornwall "Building an Entrepreneurial Culture
23 Global Entrepreneurship Monitor p.112
24 Sedov: The EY G20 Entrepreneurship Barometer 2013 p. 4
25 Burrow: The Limits of State Action p.36

Moreover, the expert rating of the entrepreneurial Eco-System of Entrepreneurship education at school stage was rated as 2.7 in a scoring system of 1- 9 whereby 1 is considered as highly insufficient. The average score is 3.1. In direct comparison to 62 other countries, Germany reaches the 40th rank. In addition, another table displays the entrepreneurial education at post school stage. In this category, Germany is once more below average, and ranks the 49th position[26] (Kelley). A connection can be drawn between entrepreneurial success and education expenditures as a percentage of GDP. Germany is the country second from the bottom in comparison to 15 others. The top three countries in this area are New Zealand, USA and the United Kingdom. In order to an improved economic education, a higher investment in e.g. electronic devices and training programs for teachers would be one step in the right direction.

In conclusion, Germany is failing to provide children with entrepreneurial skills and knowledge in analysing real-life situations while understanding the basics of economics and financial relationships. The second school curriculum has achieved especially disappointing scores although a survey in 2012 has revealed that 76% of the school children were keen to get to learn business related topics[27] (Bittorf). Recapitulating these issues of Germany, the founding country, the fertile ground for a proficient founding country is not provided. The entrepreneurial spirit is not furthered and encouraged. These interventions have consequences for the future – promising entrepreneurs may never find entrepreneurship as a possible career option. The very first step in particular is the economic and financial education in school.

---

26 Global Entrepreneurship Monitor p. 73
27 e.g. Bittorf: KFW ECONOMIC RESEARCH, p.4

3.2. Culture
3.2.1. Culture America

What does it mean "To be an entrepreneur"? Yes, these people are developers of their own ideas and are therefore their own bosses. For them there is no such thing as being below the top of the hierarchy in the company. However, being an entrepreneur also requires the mental stability, flexibility and creativity to sovereign the process of creating something from the basics of knowledge. This basic concept exists on all seven continents due to the fact that the concept of entrepreneurship has never changed. However, the view that people hold on entrepreneurship differs in every country. You could even presume a change from region to region. In some countries it just seems simpler to establish a company than in others. People would estimate that the reason for this presumption is the disparity in the countries' policies that circumscribe the entrepreneur's potential and feasibility to build a business (access to venture capital, market factors).

These two aspects are partially true. What in generally is often underestimated is the culture's mind-set on business-creation. If the career choice "entrepreneurship" is valid and respected, it is more likely that people will start a business. It is true that decision-making often interferes with what people will think of their choices. Therefore, it is crucial that a country allows for the belief that being an entrepreneur to be socially accepted. And more: Even if a bankruptcy is the outcome of a failed business, the founder should be encouraged to learn from the mistakes and start again with success being the sole destination. This is of high importance as second-time entrepreneurs show a higher rate of success than first-time entrepreneurs. "A lot of countries have a really poor public policy when it comes to bankruptcy. If we want people to take risk, then we have to think through what are the consequences of what would happen if they would fail for their families and for their future"[28]

In addition, women, young people and foreigners can make a huge contribution to the process of innovation and can broaden the entrepreneurial base – but are often underrepresented. When both Americans as well as foreign people think about the American Dream, they have a bright picture in mind in which everything can be accomplished – just being able to work hard and continuously is enough for success to be achieved. America is a country of immigration. The figures speak for themselves: In December 2015, there were 61 million immigrants living in the United States. Compared to a

---

28 Eric Ries, a Silicon Valley entrepreneur, http://www.mckinsey.com/industries/high-tech/our-insights/disruptive-entrepreneurs-an-interview-with-eric-ries 2.2.17

Native American, an immigrant is more likely to start a business. 27.5% percent of all new entrepreneurs in the United States are immigrants[29] (Robert W. Fairlie). This outstandingly high rate is due to the wide spread cultural belief of having many opportunities to gain prosperity after fleeing poverty. This culture is a decisive pull factor for America and is of high importance. There is a correlation of a low unemployment rate and a high rate of start-ups. Entrepreneurialism is rooted in America's history. Americans are proud of their cultural norm that people are comfortable with risk-taking. Moreover, they hold the belief that "their fate is in their own hands".

Another important aspect is as follows: The above-mentioned fear of failure is low. In Silicon Valley, failure is even a sign of hard work and is awarded with "social honours"[30]. The acceptance of risk taking and even failure is a characteristic of the American Dream. This leads to the assertion that the failure valid experience that will have its positivity in the next project. In Silicon Valley especially, it seems like such a thing like "failure" does not exists[31] (Almeida). And that is what makes the Cluster at the center of the American Dream. "Independency, creativity, assertive behavior, ingenuity, stubbornness, long hours and hard work" are traits essential to an entrepreneur's success– failure and triumph are subordinate parts of minor importance[32].

On the other hand, not to glorify this cultural mentality, entrepreneurs in such a surrounding tend to be unrealistic about success. They seek the best but if the outcome is shifted to being less important, the risk of failure seems higher. In the end, it is an interference between both being realistic and being very ambitious.

3.2.2. Culture Germany

"The entrepreneur is one who is willing to bear the risk of a new venture if there is a significant chance for profit."[33] This describes how entrepreneurs have to deal with the uncertainty of success or failure. However, the risk of failure and the consequential monetary loss is what the society gets suspicious of. Facts and figures confirm this issue. The Delphi-Study investigates the entrepreneurial culture of Germany. 58% of the participants hold the view that founders are socially regarded as critical and 47% indicate that Germans are risk-averse and in addition prefer a permanent employment[34]

---

29 Fairlie: "The Kauffmann Index" p.13
30 economist.com/node; "The United State of Entrepreneurs" Mar 12th 2009; 24.2.17)
31 Almeida: "To fail and to success: an entrepreneurial culture is Europe's ultimate Business Challenge"
32 ww1.jamesabruzzo.net/wp-content/uploads May 18th 2001; 24.2.17
33 https://www.ait.org.tw/infousa/zhtw/DOCS/enterp.pdf, Principles Of Entrepreneurship, U.S. Department of State/Bureau of International Information Programs, 23.2.17
34 Pinkwart: Analyse des Gründungsgeschehens in Deutschland p.8

(Pinkwart). Another study reinforces the issue of a poor entrepreneurial culture. Germany ranks poorly on the 41st rank on a total of 62 ranks under the aspect of cultural and social norms. With a value of 4.2 points, the European country is significantly below average with 4.7 points.

Particularly the insufficient "culture of failure" is a crucial issue. The Delphi-Study presents that 79% of the participants believe that this is a problem of the German culture. A "culture of second chances" and a "can do attitude" does not exist. This means that on the one hand the entrepreneur who has failed is less likely to start a new business. However, this attitude is regarded as unprofitable as people are more likely to run a successful business on the second or third attempt. "Mistakes exist to learn from them" This common saying is of high importance – but the population refuses to give the entrepreneurs second chances, hence the entrepreneurs do not feel supported by the environment.

This mind-set steers people towards more critical thinking, nonetheless more than 89% are positively convinced that they have made the right decision and are content with their current situation in the business[35] (Pinkwart). Usually, the skepticism dissolves. This social issue is a barrier to a successful start-up business career – even on the second, third or fourth attempt. A social shift has to happen to open the gates for a more favorable choice to be an entrepreneur.

4. Conclusion

Both the Unites States and Germany hold advantages and disadvantages which makes a clear-cut decision complicated. Every enterprise is different – that is why each upcoming business owner has to decide whether a relocation would promise better frame conditions. After having examined the frame condition, a predominant factor is the size of the country. Due to the fact that America is the bigger country, it provides more markets and is especially favorable for firms with niche products. On the contrary, it is a greater challenge to commercialise a product that has already been innovated. However, when a start-up has established the service or product in America, it is the chance to grow quickly. In both countries, innovation is encouraged by the government. The striking difference is that in America the children are fed with heroic stories about successful entrepreneurs like Steve Jobs and Bill Gates. Being an entrepreneurs is more celebrated in the Unites States. It is predominant that an American person is

---

35 Pinlwart: Analyse des Gründungsgeschehens in Deutschland p.9

more likely to start a business because the social surrounding is in general more encouraging.

To draw a final statement, the framework conditions in both countries are of a very high and developed standard. However, what makes a difference on the bottom-line is the culturally determined attitude to entrepreneurship and to the entrepreneurs, which is mainly due to differences in the scholastic education. That makes the Unites States country number one, where the feeling of the land of "milk and honey" still exists and in which the change "From rags to riches" can happen.

5. Summary

The extended paper gives answers to the question "From rags to riches"? Differences and parallels as regards the foundation and future development of American and German enterprises. The content is divided into the two central aspects "Frame Conditions" and "Society and Culture". These factors play an important role as they have a major impact on the entrepreneurs and the founding scene. The Unites States is a large country with many prospering markets. Moreover, the infrastructure is extended, the degree of innovation is high and the cluster structure is widely spread which is positive for the economy. Due to trade agreements the entrepreneurs are enabled to distribute their innovations to the world. Germany is central European country with a stable economy. On the one hand, Germany has positive relationships to other countries through trade agreements, on the other hand, the entrepreneurs benefit from the extensive infrastructure. The degree of innovation is still rising. America business scene in influenced by the immigrants who influence the entrepreneurial spirit in the country. The numbers show that a person who has a college degree is more likely to start a business - but also people with a basic scholastic degree make an impact. In Germany, the business career "self-employment" is especially prosperous for middle-aged people. With the large difference in the percentage of men and women, Germany is behind of most countries (for example the United States). The median entrepreneur has a higher scholastic degree which is a positive contribution to the founding of innovation based start-ups. America enhances due to investments, guiding students towards the career option of economics but giving them the freedom to choose based in their interest, the spirit of the American Dream. Germany scores poorly in the international comparison of schools concerning entrepreneurial skills. In America the career choice "entrepreneur" is respected and the self-employed are encouraged in their activity. The cultural belief is that "if you work hard you will prosper". In comparison to Germany, a bankruptcy is not seen as a failure. Germany's founding culture is considered as insufficient. To make the saying "From rags to Riches" true, the German citizens have to change their mind-set toward being encouraging even if a bankruptcy occurs.

Bibliography

Almeida, Francisca. " "to fail and to success: an entrepreneurial culture is Europe's ultimate Business Challenge"." 7 November 2014. *gmfus.org.* 16 January 2017.

Ascher, W. et al. *Physical Infrastructure Development: Balancing the Growth, Equity, and Environmental Imperatives.* Palgrave Macmillan, 2010.

Bittorf, Dr Matthias. "Germany's entrepreneurial culture: strengths and weaknesses ." December 2013. *https://www.kfw.de/PDF/Download-Center/Konzernthemen/Research/PDF-Dokumente-Fokus-Volkswirtschaft/Fokus-englische-Dateien/Fokus-Nr.-39-Dezember-2013_EN.pdf.* 22 January 2017.

Burrow, J.W. *The Limits of State Action .* Liberty Fund Inc, 1993.

Byrne, Edmond. "ENHANCING ENGINEERING EMPLOYABILITY IN THE 21st CENTURY; HANDLING UNCERTAINTY AND COMPLEXITY THROUGH 'NEW ENTREPRENEURSHIP' ." July 2012. *https://www.ucc.ie/en/media/academic/processengineering/publicationspresentations/ByrneISEE2012NewEntrepreneurship.pdf.* 27 March 2017.

"comparative indicators of education in the United States and other G-20 countries." December 2015. *https://nces.ed.gov/pubs2016/2016100.pdf.* 19 January 2017.

Conway, Steve. *Managing and shaping innovation.* Oxford, England: Oxford University Press, 2009.

Cornwall, Jeff. "Building an Entrepreneurial Culture." 1 August 2011. *www.businessinsider/fostering-an-entrepreneurial-culture.* 5 February 2017.

Federal Ministry for Economic affairs and Energy. *Start - ups and entrepreneurial spirit in Germany.* PDF. Berlin, Germany: Federal Ministry for Economic affairs and Energy, 2016.

"Germany Country Factfile." 2016. *http://www.euromonitor.com/germany/country-factfile.* 6 January 2017.

Kelley, Donna et al. "GEM Global Report." 5 2 2016. *http://www.gemconsortium.org/report/49480.* 22 Februrary 2017.

Metzger, Dr Georg. "KfW-Start-up Monitor 2016 ." 2016. *https://www.kfw.de/PDF/Download-Center/Konzernthemen/Research/PDF-Dokumente-Gr%C3%BCndungsmonitor/Gr%C3%BCndungsmonitor-englische-Dateien/KfW-Gr%C3%BCndungsmonitor-2016_EN.pdf.* 2 March 2017.

Office of the United States Trade Representative. "Executive Office Of The President." 2013. *https://ustr.gov/map/countriesaz/de.* 18 January 2016.

Owen, Eugene. n.d.

Pinkwart, Prof. Dr. Andreas. "Analyse des Gründungsgeschehen in Deutschland." 2016. *http://www.hhl.de/fileadmin/texte/publikationen/studien/LS_Innovation/Analyse_des_Gruendungsgeschehens_in_Deutschland.pdf.* 3 Februrary 2017.

Robert W. Fairlie, Arnobio Morelix, E.J. Reedy Joshua Russell. "The Kauffman Index." 2015. *http://www.kauffman.org/~/media/kauffman_org/research%20reports%20and%20covers/2015/05/kauffman_index_startup_activity_national_trends_2015.pdf.* 12 January 20217.

Röhl, Klaus-Heiner. "Entrepreneurial culture and start-ups ." 28 January 2016. *file:///C:/Users/elisa/Downloads/Entrepreneurial_culture_IW_policy_paper%20(2).pdf.* 17 March 2017.

Rosenberg, Nathan. *Inside the Black Box: Technology and Economics.* England: Cambridge University Press, 1982.

Schumpeter, J. A. *The theory of economic development: An inquiry into profits, capital, credit, interest, and the business cycle .* United States, 1934.

Schwab, Klaus. "The Global Competitiveness Report ." 2012-2013. *http://www3.weforum.org/docs/WEF_GlobalCompetitivenessReport_2012-13.pdf.* 5 March 2017.

Sedov, Viktor et al. "EY 20 Entrepreneurship Barometer 2013." 2013. *http://www.ey.com/Publication/vwLUAssetsPI/The_EY_G20_Entrepreneurship_Barometer_2013/$FILE/EY-G20-main-report.pdf.* 16 February 2017.

Sternberg, Rolf et al. "GEM- Länderbericht Deutschland." 2014. *https://www.wigeo.uni-hannover.de/fileadmin/wigeo/Geographie/Forschung/Wirtschaftsgeographie/Forschungsprojekte/laufende/GEM_2014/gem2014.pdf.* 17 January 2017.

U.S. DEPARTMENT OF EDUCATION. "Comparative Indicators of Education in the United States and Other G-20 Countries." December 2015. *https://nces.ed.gov/pubs2016/2016100.pdf.* 24 January 2017.

Woetzel, J., Garemo, N., Mischke, J., Hjerpe, M. und Palter, R. "https://www.mckinsey.de/files/mgi_bridgingglobal_infrastructure_gaps_june_2016.pdf." June 2016. *Bridging Global Infrastructure Gaps.* 4 February 2017.

Wolinski, John et al. *AQA A Level Business 1 Third Edition .* Hodder Education, 2015 . textbook.

World Economic Forum. *GCI Competitiveness Rankings.* 2016. Chart. 2 2 2017.

YOUR KNOWLEDGE HAS VALUE

- We will publish your bachelor's and master's thesis, essays and papers

- Your own eBook and book - sold worldwide in all relevant shops

- Earn money with each sale

Upload your text at www.GRIN.com
and publish for free